YEAR 3

NAPLAN*-style LANGUAGE CONVENTIONS

Do you need to go back to the basics and practise language conventions for NAPLAN? Let's read together and learn.

Parents and carers are encouraged to read the explanation and practice sections with their child.

Stella Tarakson

Illustrated by
Janice Bowles

*This is not an officially endorsed publication of the NAPLAN program and is produced by Pascal Press independently of Australian Governments.

About this book

This book is designed to review the skills required for the Language Conventions component of the year 3 NAPLAN* test and to practise NAPLAN-style questions.

The book commences with a pre-test, to help identify any areas of weakness that may require special attention.

It is then divided into three sections: spelling, grammar and punctuation. Each section is composed of eight units.

Each unit begins with a brief explanation of a particular concept. This is followed by examples of how this concept is used **(We practise)**. Practical exercises are then provided to give your child the opportunity to practise the concept **(You practise)**. These exercises reinforce the concept and check that your child understands it fully.

We recommend that your child take the eight-page pull-out test under timed conditions, once the bulk of the book has been successfully completed.

If further instruction is required, we recommend that this book be provided to your child's teacher for review. Then the parent or carer and the teacher can devise a plan to ensure all the basic contents are fully understood and consolidated.

Meet 'BOB' – Back Of the Book

At the end of each unit, BOB reminds your child to go to the Answers section at the back of the book.

Contents & Checklist

INTRODUCTION to NAPLAN*

The National Assessment Program for Literacy and Numeracy (NAPLAN) is a Federal Government initiative that requires the assessment of skills in literacy and numeracy across all Australian schools for students in years 3, 5, 7 and 9. It was introduced in 2008 to replace the previous state-based assessment programs.

NAPLAN is held annually in May. All students receive an individualised report on their performance, which can be compared to the average performance of all students in Australia. The report contains a description of each assessment area, and identifies the skills being assessed.

Using this book to prepare for the NAPLAN test

The NAPLAN Language Conventions test covers Spelling, Grammar and Punctuation and is largely based on multiple-choice questions. Students are required to identify the correct answer to a question by shading the correct bubble. Some questions, require written answers.

The units in this book are divided into three sections — spelling, grammar and punctuation — and are based on previous NAPLAN tests.

Pre-Test

A Pre-Test has been included on pages 6–7 to help you identify your child's areas of weakness. Once completed, use the marking grid on page 7 to guide you to the units that will be most helpful. Answers are supplied on page 62.

Mini-Tests

The Spelling, Grammar and Punctuation sections are each followed by two Mini-Tests. We recommend that your child take a Mini-Test every time they complete four units. Check your child's results by looking at the answers at the back of the book, and discuss any incorrect ones with them.

Pull-out test

This book comes with an eight-page removable Sample NAPLAN test. This will give your child a good idea of what to expect during the actual exam.
The results will provide the information you need to pinpoint areas that require attention. We recommend that your child take this test under timed conditions when the bulk of the book has been successfully completed.

*This is not an officially endorsed publication of the NAPLAN program and is produced by Pascal Press independently of Australian Governments.

HINTS and TIPS

Exam equipment:

* Make sure you have at least TWO sharp HB or 2B pencils—in case one breaks.
* Make sure you have an eraser—in case you mark the wrong bubble by mistake.

Reading time:

* Read all the instructions carefully.
* Read each question TWICE so you understand exactly what is being asked.

Answering multiple-choice questions:

* First, try to answer the question without looking at the choices. Once you think you know the correct answer, read through the choices.
* Fill in the answer bubble properly

  like this 

  NOT like this 

Timing:

* You will have 40 minutes to do the NAPLAN* paper, which will have about 50 questions. This means you will have less than a minute per answer.
* The paper is divided into two parts, which are worth equal marks. Aim to spend 20 minutes on each part.
* Work steadily through the questions, without rushing or dawdling. Don't be put off by an answer that seems too obvious or too simple.
* Start at question 1 and work through the questions in order. If you jump about too much, you risk accidentally missing a question.
* Temporarily skip any questions that you cannot do, rather than spending a long time on them. You might run out of time to do the easier questions!
* After you have worked through all the questions, return to any that you skipped earlier and have another go at answering them.

Review:

* Go back and check your answers if you have time at the end.
* Don't change an answer unless you are sure it is wrong!

Tricky questions:

* Look carefully at the answers. Are there any that you know are wrong? Change them!
* If you can't answer a difficult question — guess!

PRE-TEST

This pre-test can help identify areas of weakness that need extra attention. The unit or units in this book that each question relates to are identified.

SPELLING

Each sentence has one word that is incorrect. Write the correct spelling in the box.

1. The theif was caught by the police. *(Unit 1)*
2. We walked across the wobbly brige. *(Unit 2)*
3. Tom's hurtful remark was thougtles. *(Units 3 & 5)*
4. The homework was full of misstakess. *(Units 4 & 6)*
5. Do you like my new harecutt? *(Units 7 & 8)*

GRAMMAR

For questions 6 to 11, shade the bubble of the word which completes the sentence correctly.

6. Dimitri was proud of himself when ____ won an award. *(Unit 9)*
   - ○ them
   - ○ it
   - ○ he
   - ○ they

7. I'll throw the ball and you try to ____ it. *(Units 10 & 11)*
   - ○ catch
   - ○ catched
   - ○ caught
   - ○ catching

8. The birds ____ across the sky. *(Unit 12)*
   - ○ fly
   - ○ flies

9. Kate is the ____ swimmer in her class. *(Unit 13)*
   - ○ strong
   - ○ stronger
   - ○ strongest

10. My dog dug a hole ____ the fence. *(Unit 14)*
    - ○ in
    - ○ under
    - ○ through
    - ○ at

11. Why do you like tennis ____ not squash? *(Units 15 & 16)*
    - ○ and
    - ○ if
    - ○ but
    - ○ then

PRE-TEST

PUNCTUATION

For questions 12 to 14, shade the bubble of the sentence with correct punctuation.

12

- ⬭ It is sharon's birthday tomorrow Are you going to the party?
- ⬭ It is Sharon's birthday tomorrow. Are you going? to the party.
- ⬭ It is Sharon's birthday tomorrow? are you going to the party.
- ⬭ It is Sharon's birthday tomorrow. Are you going to the party? *(Units 17 & 18)*

13

- ⬭ My best friends are Vicky Jia, and Susan.
- ⬭ My best friends, are Vicky Jia and Susan.
- ⬭ My best friends are Vicky, Jia and Susan.
- ⬭ My best friends, are Vicky, Jia and Susan. *(Units 19 & 20)*

14

- ⬭ "It's too hot in here, Dean said".
- ⬭ "It's too hot in here Dean said."
- ⬭ "It's too hot in here", Dean said.
- ⬭ "It's too hot in here," Dean said. *(Units 21 & 22)*

15

Where does the missing apostrophe (') go? Shade ONE bubble.

BOB time!

(Units 23 & 24)

MARKING GRID

Question	Unit	Skill	Correct/Incorrect
1	1	Rules for vowels	
2	2	Rules for consonants	
3	3 & 5	Commonly misspelt words & suffixes	
4	4 & 6	Prefixes & plurals	
5	7 & 8	Homophones & compound words	
6	9	Nouns	
7	10 & 11	Verbs and tenses	
8	12	Subject and verb agreement	
9	13	Adjectives and adverbs	
10	14	Articles and prepositions	
11	15 & 16	Clauses and conjunctions & sentences	
12	17 & 18	Capital letters, full stops, question marks and exclamation marks	
13	19 & 20	Commas	
14	21 & 22	Speech marks	
15	23 & 24	Apostrophes for contraction and possession	
TOTAL			

RULES FOR VOWELS

SPELLING

The magic 'e'. The letter e at the end of a word usually makes the vowel say its name ...

cake, hive, rope, mule

... but there are exceptions!

dare, give, lose

For words with an ee sound, use i before e ...

thief, yield, believe

... except after 'c' ...

ceiling, receive, conceit

... but there are exceptions!

weird, their

The letter q is always followed by the letter u.

No exceptions.

quiet, quite, queen

Acronyms don't count as words when it comes to spelling rules e.g. *Qantas*.

Some combinations of vowels make the same sound.

au and aw	*audio, saw*
ear, eer, ere	*dear, deer, here*
ou and ow	*mouse, cow*
oar, our, ore	*boar, pour, tore*

... but there are exceptions!

there, show, hour

When two vowels go walking, the first does the talking.

That is, the first vowel says its name ...

rain, beam, tie, toe, blue

... but there are exceptions!

said, bread, cook, shoe, coin

Try following the rule first. If it looks wrong, it might be an exception.

We practise

Write the correct spelling for the circled word in the box.

My little brother went to play in the (rane).	rain
He (caym) back soaking wet.	came
Mum (qwickly) changed his clothes.	quickly
Now he's caught an (auful) cold.	awful

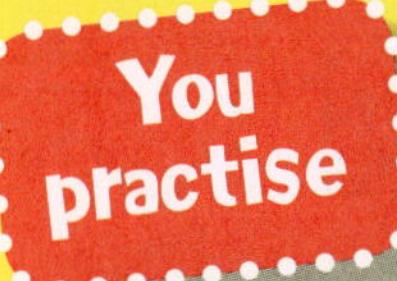

Write the correct spelling for the circled word in the box.

1 Rachel ran arownd the garden.

2 The theif was caught by the police.

3 The qeen is wearing her crown.

4 I love to flote in the swimming pool.

5 Do not be decieved by the trick.

You practise

One word is incorrect. Write the correct spelling in the box.

6 Would you like to come to my howse?

7 Dad put a frypan on the stoav.

8 It is very hot heer today.

9 It is such a releif now the test is over.

10 "Please be qwiet," the teacher said.

RULES FOR CONSONANTS

These rules apply for consonants at the **end** of words.

In words that end in 'y', the 'y' often makes a long ee sound ...

happy, baby, monkey

... but the 'y' makes a long 'i' sound if there are no vowels in the word.

sky, cry, try

If you hear a 'ch' sound after a short vowel, it is spelled tch ...

hatch, witch, clutch

... but there are exceptions!

rich, much

If you hear a 'k' after a short vowel, it is spelled ck ...

duck, back, sock

... but there are exceptions!

magic, epic

If you hear a 'j' sound after a short vowel, it is spelled dge ...

badge, bridge, edge

... but if it comes after a long vowel, it is spelled 'ge'.

rage, cage

Rules can help, but keep exceptions in mind!

We practise

Write the correct spelling of the circled word in the box.

Julie has a new little (puppie).	puppy
She is teaching him to (fech) a stick.	fetch
One day he got (stuk) in the mud.	stuck
He tries to eat Julie's chocolate (fuge).	fudge

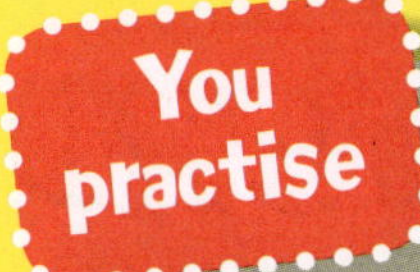

Write the correct spelling of the circled word in the box.

1. The wicked wich cast a spell.
2. Ali has a new babee brother.
3. The budgie flew out of its caje.
4. Naomi was in trouble for throwing stiks.
5. Peeling onions makes me crie.

You practise

One word is incorrect. Write the correct spelling in the box.

6. Dina wants to be a truk driver.
7. Jason's rash started to ich.
8. The juge sat in the courtroom.
9. The bird flew across the skie.
10. I am happie to meet you at last.

BOB time!

COMMONLY MISSPELT WORDS

Words ending in a shun sound can be spelled in different ways.

The 'shun' sound is often written 'tion'.

station, nation, election

It may also be written 'sion'.

discussion, profession

If the word refers to a person's job, the sound is usually written 'cian'.

musician, magician

The letters ough can be pronounced in many different ways.

dough	long 'o' sound
through	'oo' sound
cough	'off' sound
rough	'uff' sound
thought	'aw' sound
bough	'ow' sound

The best way to learn to spel tricky words is to practise!

Silent letters are letters that you cannot hear when you pronounce a word.

Words starting with a 'n' sound sometimes have a silent 'k' at the beginning. *knife, kneel, knuckle*

Words starting with a 'r' sound sometimes have a silent 'w' at the beginning. *write, wrong, wrist*

Words ending with a 'm' sound sometimes have a silent 'b' at the end. *thumb, crumb, lamb*

Words ending with a 'k' or 'd' sound sometimes have a silent 'l' before the last letter. *folk, yolk, could, would*

We practise

Write the correct spelling of the circled word in the box.

It rained so hard we thawt it would never stop.	thought
Two days of rain felt more than enuff.	enough
We did not now it was a very good thing.	know
It meant the drowt was finally over!	drought

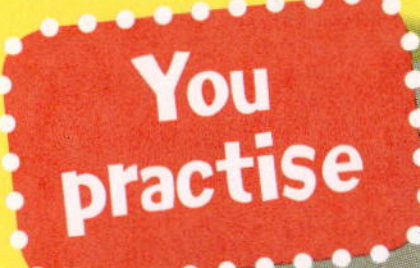

Write the correct spelling of the circled word in the box.

1 I really shood learn to spell better.

2 Toss the rapper in the bin.

3 The electrishun fixed the lights.

4 Sanjiv suffers from moshun sickness.

5 The overcooked steak was too tuff.

You practise

One word is incorrect. Write the correct spelling in the box.

6 The sign on the ice cream van said: 'Cawtion, children'.

7 The pigs wallowed in the troff.

8 The handsome night rescued the princess.

9 I am very good at subtraction and addishun.

10 Do you like my new rist watch?

PREFIXES

A prefix is a group of letters added to the beginning of a word. It makes a new word. Often the new word has the opposite meaning to the base word.

un + true = *untrue*

dis + appear = *disappear*

in + sane = *insane*

The prefix 're' means something is done again or repeated.

re + do = *redo*

When adding a prefix, the spelling of the base word does not change.

Common prefixes include:

Hint: often the last letter of the prefix is the same as the first letter of the base word.

legal	*illegal*
regular	*irregular*

But this is not always the case!

reliable	*unreliable*

Write the correct spelling and correct prefix for the circled word in the box.

Dad had to unfrost the meat before we could cook it.	defrost
It is my job to empty the decycle bin once a week.	recycle
Sammy unplaced her glasses and now she can't find them.	misplaced
I hope the magician reeappears soon!	reappears

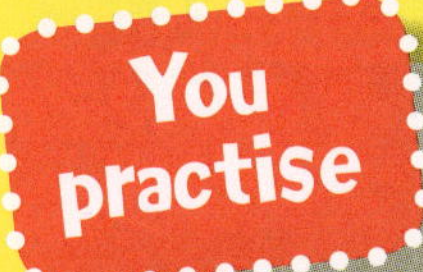

Write the correct spelling and correct prefix for the circled word in the box.

1 The burglar crept away unnseen.

2 I'm sorry, but I dissagree.

3 Cheryl unlikes broccoli.

4 Ibrahim dezipped his jacket.

5 Can you reeplay that song?

You practise

One word is incorrect. Write it in the box with the correct spelling and correct prefix.

6 Tommy had to reewrite his story five times.

7 It was a misstake anyone could make.

8 The balloon began to unflate.

9 Jennifer delocked the front door.

10 Alessio's bedroom is very mistidy.

Now try the spelling test on page 24!

BOB time!

UNIT 5

SUFFIXES

A suffix is a letter or group of letters added to the end of a word.

It makes a new word. Often the spelling of the base word does not change when a suffix is added.

use + ful = *useful*

However, sometimes the base word changes when a suffix is added:

last letter consonant – second last letter vowel – double the last letter

run + ing = *running*

last letter 'y' – change the 'y' to 'i'

happy + est = *happiest*

last letter silent 'e' – remove the 'e'

make + ing = *making*

There are always exceptions to the rules – try not to be tricked!

Common suffixes include:
s, es, ed, er, est, ful, ing, ish, ly, less.

We practise

Write the correct spelling and correct suffix for the circled word in the box.

I am the younging person in my family.	youngest
Serena left the room quickful.	quickly
Georgina and I walkes to school yesterday.	walked
The little puppy was fretest for its owner.	fretting
The handsome knight was a fearish fighter.	fearless

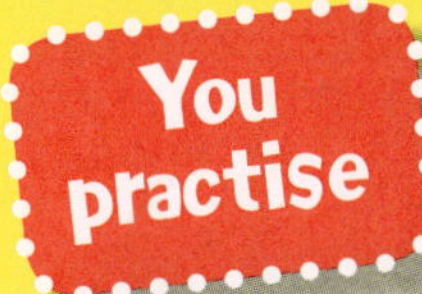

Write the correct spelling and correct suffix for the circled word in the box.

1 Oscar is cleanning his room.

2 Forget it, it's a hopeles task.

3 I'm feeling very cheerfull today.

4 That's the uglyful dog I've ever seen.

5 I am feeling hopful about the contest.

You practise

One word is incorrect. Write the correct spelling and correct suffix in the box.

6 Huan walked away sadlee.

7 That's the funniful joke I've ever heard!

8 My little brother now dressers himself in the morning.

9 This is turnning out to be a good day.

10 The sun is shining brightlie.

BOB time!

PLURALS

For many words, to make a plural you simply add s to the end of the word.

duck	*ducks*
building	*buildings*
table	*tables*

If a word ends in s, x, ch or sh, add es to the end to make it plural.

bus	*buses*
fox	*foxes*
torch	*torches*
bush	*bushes*

Some words change their vowel sound when they become a plural.

They include:

man	*men*
tooth	*teeth*
goose	*geese*

Some words change even more!

child	*children*
person	*people*

If a word ends in y and if the letter before the 'y' is a vowel add s ...

toy	*toys*

... but if the letter before the y is a consonant, remove the 'y' and add ies.

baby	*babies*

Look carefully at the last letter of the word when making plurals.

We practise

Write the correct spelling for the circled word in the box.

The foxs crept up to the chicken coop.	foxes
They wanted to steal some egges.	eggs
All the chicken started to flap and squawk.	chickens
The boies came out and chased the foxes away.	boys

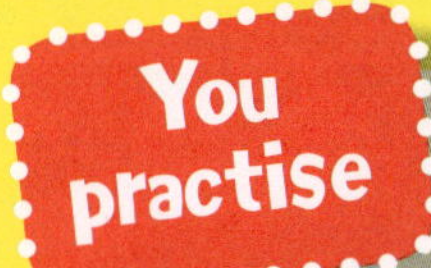

Write the correct spelling for the circled word in the box.

1 Grandma has false tooths.

2 The babys started to cry.

3 The gooses honked loudly.

4 Ken is playing with his new toies.

5 We visited two beachs in one day.

You practise

One word is incorrect. Write the correct spelling in the box.

6 The soccer coachs cheered the loudest.

7 The flys buzzed around our food.

8 I love books with puzzles and quizzs.

9 We forgot to pack the toothbrushs.

10 Have you seen my car keyes?

HOMOPHONES

Homophones are words that sound the same but have a different spelling. They mean different things.

Pay attention to the context – that is, what does the word mean in the sentence you are reading? Read the whole sentence.

Eddie's **hair** is too long.

The **hare** was very quick.

The **sea** was rough.

Can you **see** me?

I am proud of my **son**.

The **sun** is hot today.

Sounds very interesting!

We practise

Which homophone is correct? Write it in the box.

My little sister is too/two years old.	two
She is not allowed/aloud to play outside by herself.	allowed
She might fall over and get a sore/saw knee.	sore
She might be stung by a be/bee and start to cry.	bee

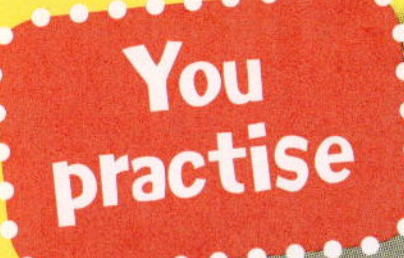

Which homophone is correct? Write it in the box.

1 We are having meet/meat for dinner.

2 I knew/new the answer to the question.

3 The birthday girl blew/blue out the candles.

4 Don't drop the vase, it might break/brake!

5 Timothy walked by/buy the shop.

You practise

One word is incorrect. Write the correct spelling in the box.

6 Leon eight dinner at his cousin's house.

7 It is rude to stair at people.

8 I'd rather eat an apple than a pair.

9 Yianni is sick at home with the flew.

10 Have you herd of Jersey cows?

UNIT 8

COMPOUND WORDS

A compound word is made when two smaller words join up to form a new word.

The spelling of the smaller words does not change. All that changes is that there is now no space between them.

sun + shine = *sunshine*

If you can spell the small words, you can also spell the compound words!

The meaning of the new word is usually related to the original two words ...

bird + house = *birdhouse*

... but sometimes it can be very different!

butter + fly = *butterfly*

Not all words with more than one syllable are compound words.

These words are not compound words ...

finger, water

... but can be made into compound words by adding other words.

fingerprint, waterfall

Use the words in the list to make new compound words. Write the new word in the box.

sun, yard, man, set

back + ________ = backyard

________ + rise = sunrise

sun + ________ = sunset

snow + ________ = snowman

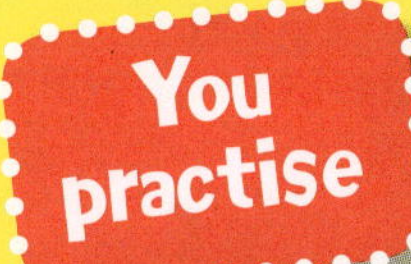

**Use the words in the list to make new compound words.
Write the new word in the box.**

skate, snake, sand, melon, light

1. rattle + ________ [ ]

2. water + ________ [ ]

3. ________ + board [ ]

4. ________ + paper [ ]

5. day + ________ [ ]

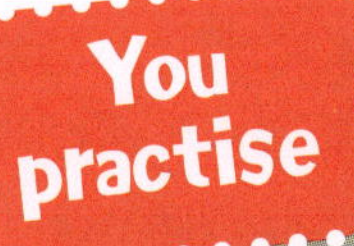

**One word is incorrect.
Write the correct spelling in the box.**

6. Can I ask you sumthing? [ ]

7. Mum is going to paint my bedroum next weekend. [ ]

8. Eleni got wet because she could not find her raincote. [ ]

9. David was feeling very homesic. [ ]

10. My little sister asked Mum for a nightlite. [ ]

Now try the spelling test on page 25!

You practise

SPELLING TEST 1

Do this test after completing Unit 4. Spend no more than 8 minutes on it.

The spelling mistake in each sentence has been circled. Write the correct spelling in the box.

1. The cieling was painted with stars.
2. The toy bote began to sink.
3. Jamal ate a tuna sandwitch.
4. We went to the railway stashun.
5. I've had enuff to eat.

Each sentence has one word that is incorrect. Write the correct spelling in the box.

6. Giovanna did not beleive the rumour.
7. Would you like to mayk a paper hat?
8. The monkee ate a banana.
9. Have a look threw that window.
10. Cheryl scraped her nee.

BOB time!

SPELLING TEST 2

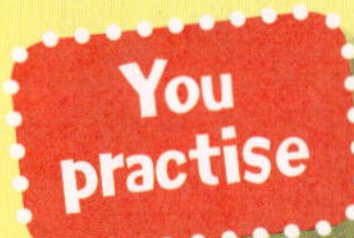

Do this test after completing Unit 8. Spend no more than 8 minutes on it.

The spelling mistake in each sentence has been circled. Write the correct spelling in the box.

1 This will be our weeklee task.

2 Daryl was so surprised, he was speechles.

3 The ball was lost among the bushs.

4 I am going to join the school banned.

5 Would you like a vanilla milkshayk?

Each sentence has one word that is incorrect. Write the correct spelling in the box.

6 His scraped knee was very painfull.

7 The movie was long but enjoyeble.

8 Jasmine one the race easily.

9 The witchs cast a magic spell.

10 I am growing sunflours in my garden.

BOB time!

UNIT 9

NOUNS

GRAMMAR

A noun is a naming word. There are different types of nouns.

Common nouns name people, places, things or ideas. They do not name *particular* people, places or things, e.g. *man, city, day, war.*

Proper nouns name a particular person, place or thing. They always start with a capital letter, e.g. *Albert, Sydney, Monday, World War I.*

Nouns are usually the first words we learn!

Abstract nouns name something you cannot see, touch, hear, smell or feel – such as an emotion or an idea, e.g. *love, sleep, peace.*

Pronouns can replace proper nouns, e.g. *he, she, I, we, you, they.* Pronouns have to match the noun in terms of number, e.g. 'they were' is correct (both are plural), 'they was' is wrong ('they' is plural, 'was' is singular).

Concrete nouns name something physical that you can see, touch, hear, smell or feel, e.g. *car, girl, smoke.*

Read the text and answer the questions.

"Have you heard the joke about the two guys in the jungle?" Janice asked Pavlo.

"I'm not sure," Pavlo replied. "How does it go?"

"Well, two friends were walking in the jungle when they heard a leopard roar. They turned around and saw it chasing them. Both started to run, and one said to the other, "I'm lucky I bought these new running shoes."

"Don't be silly," his friend replied. "You can't outrun a leopard."

"I don't need to outrun the leopard. I just need to outrun you."

Find a proper noun in the text and write it in the box.

Janice

Shade ONE bubble to show your answer.

Which word from the text is a concrete noun?

- ○ silly
- ● jungle

Which word from the text is an abstract noun?

- ● joke
- ○ walking

We practise

You practise

Read the text and answer questions 1 to 3.

"I don't get it," Pavlo said. "Why does he just need to outrun his friend? The leopard can still catch him."

"Because … oh, don't worry!"

1 **Find a proper noun in the text and write it in the box.** ☐

Shade ONE bubble to show your answer.
Which word from the text is a concrete noun?

- ◯ leopard
- ◯ worry

Which word from the text is an abstract noun?

- ◯ leopard
- ◯ worry

Shade ONE bubble to show your answer.

Which word is a proper noun?

- ◯ city
- ◯ Japan
- ◯ boy
- ◯ sister

Which word is a pronoun?

- ◯ Sheryl
- ◯ he
- ◯ alligator
- ◯ London

Which word is a proper noun and should start with a capital letter?

My brother and I went to canberra last week with our cousins.

- ◯ Brother
- ◯ Canberra
- ◯ Week
- ◯ Cousins

Which word completes the sentence correctly?

The boys ran across the playground because ________ were late for school.

- ◯ them
- ◯ it
- ◯ he
- ◯ they

VERBS

A **verb** is an action word, and tells us what is happening. There are different types of verbs.

Action verbs are things that a person, animal or thing can do, e.g. *run, cry, eat.*

Saying verbs are used to show who is saying something. They can also show how it is said, e.g. *say, shout, whisper, mutter.*

Thinking verbs show different ways of thinking, e.g. *wonder, worry, believe, imagine.*

Watch out for this trap!
'Could of', 'would of', 'should of' are wrong. The correct way to use these verbs is 'could have', 'would have', 'should have'.

Sensing verbs relate to the five senses which are sight, hearing, smell, touch and taste, e.g. *see, look, hear.*

Feeling verbs show how someone is feeling or how they show their feelings, e.g. *like, love, hate, fear.*

Relating verbs identify things and show how things are linked, e.g. *have, be, become.*

We practise

Read the text and answer the questions. Shade ONE bubble.

"I'll count to ten while you go and hide," Tina said.
George, her little brother, giggled. He loved hide and seek. He ran out of the room, wondering where he could hide. Tina usually found him very quickly, so he needed to find a good hiding spot. He knew – inside the laundry hamper. She would never see him there!
George pulled out the dirty clothes, then climbed carefully into the hamper. He grabbed a dirty shirt and covered himself with it. He could hear Tina looking for him. This was so much fun!

Which word from the text is an action verb?
- ● count
- ○ out

Which word from the text is a sensing verb?
- ○ him
- ● see

Which word from the text is a relating verb?
- ● was
- ○ with

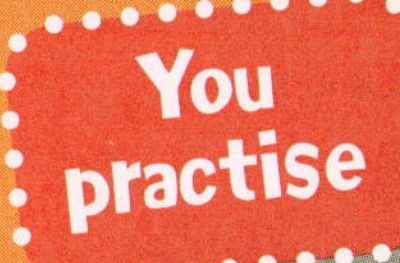

Read the text and answer questions 1 to 3.
Shade ONE bubble in each question.

George heard someone whistling. It sounded like Dad. The whistling got louder, then George heard footsteps. He giggled. He felt invisible; no one knew he was here.

But then – pong! A pair of smelly socks landed right near George's nose!

1 Which word from the text is an action verb?

- ○ whistling
- ○ louder

2 Which word from the text is a relating verb?

- ○ landed
- ○ was

3 Which word from the text is a sensing verb?

- ○ heard
- ○ whistling

4 Which word completes the sentence correctly?

I could _______ danced all night.

- ○ of
- ○ have

Which word tells the reader WHAT was done?
Shade ONE bubble in each question.

5 The cat walked gracefully across the room.

- ○ cat
- ○ walked
- ○ gracefully
- ○ room

6 Jean and Vasili rolled down the grassy hill.

- ○ Jean and Vasili
- ○ rolled
- ○ down
- ○ grassy

7 "Come and get me!" Maria shouted.

- ○ and
- ○ me
- ○ Maria
- ○ shouted

VERBS AND TENSES

Verbs are action words, e.g. *swim, like, hear.*

Tenses refer to time. A verb's tense tells **when** the action in the sentence or story is taking place. It may be in the past, present or future.

Past tense – it has already happened. Sometimes 'ed' is added to the base word, e.g. walk – *walked*.

Alex *walked* down the street.

Sometimes the base word changes completely, e.g. write – *wrote* – *written*.

Alex *wrote* a letter.

Alex *has written* a letter.

Present tense – it is happening now. Sometimes 's' is added to the base word, e.g. walk – *walks*.

Alex *walks* down the street.

Sometimes 'ing' is added to the base word, e.g. walk – *walking*.

Alex *is walking* down the street.

Future tense – it has not happened yet. The words 'will' or 'is going to' often come before the verb.

Alex *will walk* down the street.

Alex *is going to walk* down the street.

Verbs can tell us **when** things happen.

We practise

Which is the correct verb? Write it in the box.

Mark's grandfather fought/fights in World War II.	fought
The seagull eats/eaten stale bread.	eats
We will go/went to the beach next weekend.	will go

You practise Which is the correct verb? Write it in the box.

1. Lucy *fell/falls* down the stairs last week. [ ]
2. Aaron *is coming/come* over for dinner tonight. [ ]
3. Magda decided to *ride/rode* her bike to school every day. [ ]
4. Sasha *swam/swims* in the pool yesterday. [ ]
5. Harry *is doing/did* his homework right now. [ ]

You practise Which word or words complete the sentence correctly? Shade ONE bubble in each question.

6 **Jason has ________ a cold.**

- ○ catch
- ○ catched
- ○ caught
- ○ catching

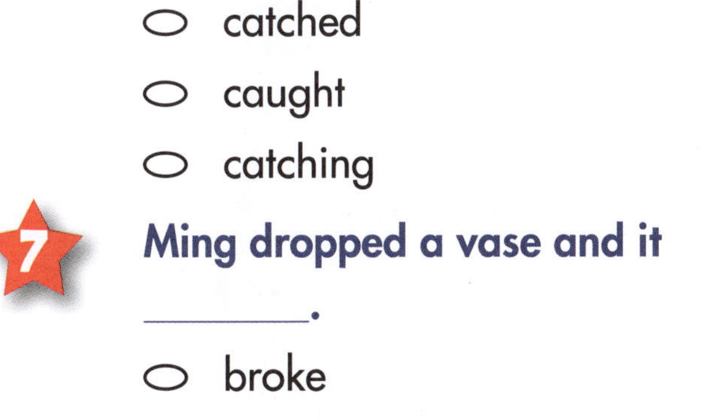

7 **Ming dropped a vase and it ________.**

- ○ broke
- ○ broken
- ○ break
- ○ breaks

8 **Tomorrow ________ a great day!**

- ○ will
- ○ will be
- ○ was
- ○ has been

9 **Dianne ________ the piano now.**

- ○ played
- ○ is playing
- ○ has played
- ○ playing

10 **The bird ________ around the room and landed on my head.**

- ○ flies
- ○ fly
- ○ flown
- ○ flew

BOB time!

SUBJECT and VERB AGREEMENT

Sentences contain a **subject** (a person or thing that does something) and a **verb** (an action word).

The subject and verb must agree.
A **singular** subject (only one) must have a singular verb.

The **dog chases** the ball.

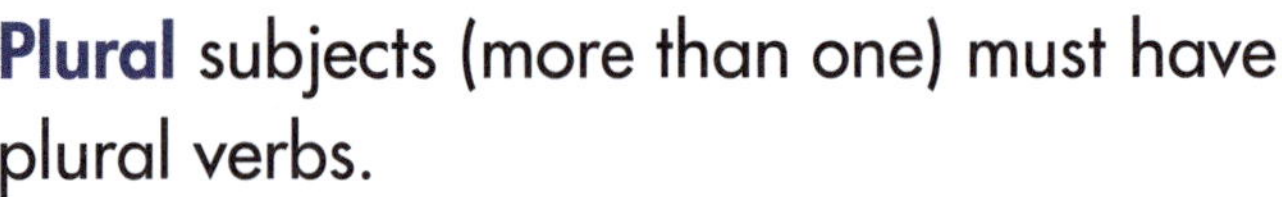

Plural subjects (more than one) must have plural verbs.

The **dogs chase** the ball.

Plural subject **Plural verb**

We practise

Which is the correct verb in each sentence? Write it in the box.

The old man sits/sit on the lounge.	sits
The children were/was taken to the museum.	were
The dogs sniffs/sniff their food.	sniff
Sophia is/are a very pretty girl.	is

You practise

Which is the correct verb in each sentence? Write it in the box.

1 The boys *run/runs* across the playground.

2 Wendy *is/are* my best friend.

3 I *was/were* helping Mum in the kitchen.

4 The girls *drink/drinks* hot chocolate.

5 The apple *taste/tastes* good.

You practise

Choose the correct verb to fill the gap. Shade ONE bubble in each question.

6 **I _____ catching the train tomorrow.**

- ⬭ am
- ⬭ are

7 **English _____ my favourite subject.**

- ⬭ is
- ⬭ are

8 **The cats _____ in the basket.**

- ⬭ is
- ⬭ are

9 **We _____ given gold stars.**

- ⬭ was
- ⬭ were

10 **The kangaroos _____ across the grass.**

- ⬭ hops
- ⬭ hop

ADJECTIVES and ADVERBS

Adjectives
describe **nouns**. They tell us things such as colour, size, shape, how many, e.g. brown, tall, round, few.

Adverbs
describe **verbs**. They tell us how, when or where an action was done, e.g. carefully, soon, above.

Adjectives help us compare things or people to each other.

When we are comparing two things, many adjectives end in 'er'.

the *taller* man

When we are comparing three or more things, many adjectives end in 'est'.

the *tallest* man

There are exceptions – *bad* and *worse* (not badder).

Adverbs can compare how things are done.

Like adjectives, when we compare two actions, many adverbs end in 'er'.

Peter jumped *higher* than Rob.

When we compare three or more actions, many adverbs end in 'est'.

Out of all the boys, Peter jumped the *highest*.

We practise

Which word completes the sentence correctly? Shade ONE bubble in each question.

My homework is usually _____.

- ● easy
- ○ easier
- ○ easiest

My homework is _____ than my brother's homework.

- ○ easy
- ● easier
- ○ easiest

My homework is the _____ I've had this year.

- ○ easy
- ○ easier
- ● easiest

You practise

Which word completes the sentence correctly?
Shade ONE bubble in each question.

1 **Stavro is _____ than his brother.**
- ⬭ small
- ⬭ smaller
- ⬭ smallest

2 **Stavro is the _____ boy in his class.**
- ⬭ small
- ⬭ smaller
- ⬭ smallest

3 **My sister Pam's hair is very _____.**
- ⬭ short
- ⬭ shorter
- ⬭ shortest

4 **Pam's hair is _____ than my hair.**
- ⬭ short
- ⬭ shorter
- ⬭ shortest

5 **Pam's hair is the _____ in our family.**
- ⬭ short
- ⬭ shorter
- ⬭ shortest

You practise

Which word tells the reader HOW an action was done?
Shade ONE bubble in each question.

6 **Neville gently picked the bird up and put it back in the cage.**
- ⬭ gently
- ⬭ picked
- ⬭ bird
- ⬭ cage

7 **The butcher carefully sliced the meat.**
- ⬭ butcher
- ⬭ carefully
- ⬭ sliced
- ⬭ meat

You practise

Choose the best adverb to complete the sentence.
Shade ONE bubble.

8 **Matt hit the ball _____.**
- ⬭ hard
- ⬭ harder
- ⬭ hardest

9 **Simon hit the ball _____ than Matt.**
- ⬭ hard
- ⬭ harder
- ⬭ hardest

10 **Belinda was stronger than the others so she hit the ball the _____.**
- ⬭ hard
- ⬭ harder
- ⬭ hardest

BOB time!

ARTICLES and PREPOSITIONS

Articles describe nouns. There are only three articles in English: a, an, the.

The article 'the' refers to a specific person, place or thing.

*Harry patted **the** dog.*

The articles 'a' and 'an' do not refer to specific people, places or things. 'An' is used for words beginning with vowels.

*Harry wished he had **a** dog.*

Don't end a sentence with a preposition!

Avoid this trap:
'Between' is used when something is in the middle of two things. 'Among' is used when there are three or more things.

Prepositions are words that give the position or location of things and people.

Mum is working **at** her computer.

↑ **preposition**

They can also tell us when something happens.

I haven't eaten **since** breakfast.

↑ **preposition**

Common prepositions include: on, in, above, under, beside, between, with, until, during, by.

We practise

Choose an article from the list to fill the gap and write it in the box.

an, a, the

Marie wants to be ____ doctor when she grows up. [a]

I have ____ kindest doctor in the world! [the]

Choose a preposition from the list to fill each gap and write it in the box.

on, after, in, under, before

I went for a run ____ the park. [in]

I have to brush my teeth ____ I go to bed. [before]

You practise Choose a preposition from the list to fill each gap and write it in the box.

under, into, between, on, over

1. The cat jumped _______ the fence. [ ]
2. We drove _______ the city. [ ]
3. Naomi sat _______ her two brothers. [ ]
4. The dog dug a hole _______ the fence. [ ]
5. Put the cup _______ the table. [ ]

You practise Which word completes the sentence correctly? Shade ONE bubble in each question.

6. Do you know _____ answer?

- ⬭ a
- ⬭ an
- ⬭ the

7. Can you give me _____ clue?

- ⬭ a
- ⬭ an
- ⬭ the

8. Don't go _____ yourself.

- ⬭ by
- ⬭ with
- ⬭ among
- ⬭ between

9. I went for a ride _____ my scooter.

- ⬭ on
- ⬭ in
- ⬭ through
- ⬭ under

10. There was dust on the floor _____ my bed.

- ⬭ in
- ⬭ under
- ⬭ through
- ⬭ at

CLAUSES and CONJUNCTIONS

A **clause** is a group of words that has a **subject** (a person or thing that does something) and a **verb** (an action).

Clauses can show what is happening and who is doing something.

Carolyn kicked the ball.

subject verb

A clause can be part of a sentence. It can also be a complete sentence because it makes sense on its own.

Phrases differ from clauses because they do not make sense on their own.

Conjunctions are joining words. They join words or clauses together to make a sentence. They can hint what is coming next in the sentence. For example, the conjunction 'and' means there is more to come. The conjunction 'but' means something different is about to be explained.

I like cats **and** *dogs,* **but** *I am not allowed to have a pet.*

We practise

Which word completes the sentence correctly? Shade ONE bubble in each question.

We will go to the park _______ it starts to rain.

- ○ if
- ● unless

Sophie would like milk and biscuits _______ she is hungry.

- ● because
- ○ but

Alex will do it, _______ he really doesn't want to.

- ● but
- ○ so

You practise Which word completes the sentence correctly? Shade ONE bubble in each question.

1 I like fish ______ chips.
- ⬭ and
- ⬭ or
- ⬭ also
- ⬭ nor

2 We will be late ______ we hurry.
- ⬭ if
- ⬭ but
- ⬭ once
- ⬭ unless

3 Either Ranjit ______ Paul will visit us today.
- ⬭ and
- ⬭ or
- ⬭ but
- ⬭ whichever

4 Dylan was late ______ he slept in.
- ⬭ if
- ⬭ although
- ⬭ until
- ⬭ because

You practise Which word completes the sentence correctly? Shade ONE bubble in each question.

5 You can come out with me ______ stay at home.
- ⬭ and
- ⬭ or
- ⬭ if
- ⬭ but

6 It's getting dark ______ we should leave.
- ⬭ so
- ⬭ or
- ⬭ though
- ⬭ why

7 Neil likes peaches ______ not plums.
- ⬭ or
- ⬭ while
- ⬭ so
- ⬭ but

8 You can have some ______ you ask nicely.
- ⬭ before
- ⬭ until
- ⬭ if
- ⬭ while

BOB time!

SENTENCES

A sentence is a group of words that has a meaning. It has a subject (a person or thing that does something) and a verb (an action).

A sentence begins with a capital letter and ends with either, a full stop, question mark or exclamation mark.

William **washed** his hands.

capital — subject — verb — full stop

There are four types of sentences:

Statement	Tells the reader something.	
	Ends with a full stop.	.
Question	Asks something.	
	Ends with a question mark.	?
Command	Orders that something be done.	
	Ends with an exclamation mark or full stop.	!
Exclamation	Shows very strong feelings.	
	Ends with an exclamation mark or full stop.	!

Which sentence is a question? Shade ONE bubble.

○ Kate shut the door.

● Did Kate shut the door?

Which sentence is a command? Shade ONE bubble.

● Shut the door, Kate!

○ Kate shut the door.

Which sentence is an exclamation? Shade ONE bubble.

● I can't believe Kate slammed the door!

○ Shut the door, Kate!

You practise

Shade ONE bubble in each question to show your answer.

In questions 1 and 2, which sentence is a command?

- ⬭ I like your new dress.
- ⬭ Would you like a biscuit?
- ⬭ Wash your hands!
- ⬭ I'm so excited!

- ⬭ Do it now!
- ⬭ How are you?
- ⬭ It is nine o'clock.
- ⬭ It's my birthday party tomorrow!

In questions 3 and 4, which sentence is an exclamation?

- ⬭ Is that a new bag?
- ⬭ I won first prize!
- ⬭ Go to bed!
- ⬭ The dog barked all night.

- ⬭ I saw a ghost!
- ⬭ Do you believe in ghosts?
- ⬭ It was a cloudy night.
- ⬭ Hurry up!

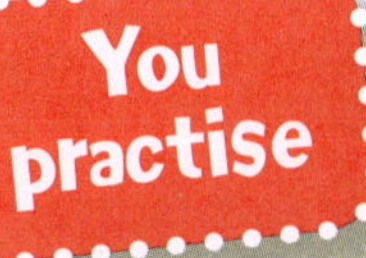

Shade ONE bubble in each question to show your answer.

In questions 5 and 6, which sentence is a question?

- ⬭ Jim lives across the road.
- ⬭ Where does Jim live?
- ⬭ Brush your teeth!
- ⬭ I'm so happy!

- ⬭ What is your favourite colour?
- ⬭ The leaves turned brown.
- ⬭ I can't wait for summer!
- ⬭ Go to your room!

In questions 7 and 8, which sentence is a statement?

- ⬭ Do you have a pet?
- ⬭ I love my little dog!
- ⬭ My dog's name is Sam.
- ⬭ Sit!

- ⬭ Mum is baking bread.
- ⬭ Would you like some fresh bread?
- ⬭ That smells delicious!
- ⬭ Eat it now!

Now try the grammar test on page 43!

BOB time!

You practise

GRAMMAR TEST 1

Do this test after completing Unit 12. Spend no more than 6 minutes on this test.

For each question, shade ONE bubble to show the correct answer.

Which word is a proper noun and should start with a capital letter?

1 **We are moving into a new house on Russell street.**

- ⬭ moving
- ⬭ new
- ⬭ house
- ⬭ street

Which word tells the reader WHAT was done?

2 **Donna sang at the school concert.**

- ⬭ Donna
- ⬭ sang
- ⬭ school
- ⬭ concert

3 **Which sentence is correct?**

- ⬭ I should of listened to you.
- ⬭ I should has listened to you.
- ⬭ I should have listened to you.
- ⬭ I should ov listened to you.

In questions 4 to 8, which word completes the sentence correctly?

4 **The dog wagged _____ tail.**

- ⬭ their
- ⬭ its
- ⬭ my

5 **Ryan _____ set the table last night.**

- ⬭ help
- ⬭ helps
- ⬭ helped
- ⬭ helping

6 **I will _____ a letter to my Grandma.**

- ⬭ write
- ⬭ written
- ⬭ wrote
- ⬭ writing

7 **The boy _____ his lunch.**

- ⬭ eat
- ⬭ eats

8 **Zhang _____ going to school.**

- ⬭ was
- ⬭ were

BOB time!

GRAMMAR TEST 2

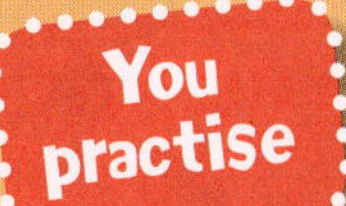

Do this test after completing Unit 16. Spend no more than 6 minutes on this test.

For each question, shade ONE bubble to show the correct answer.

Which word tells the reader HOW an action was done?

1 **Evan carefully closed the door so he wouldn't wake the sleeping baby.**

- ○ carefully
- ○ closed
- ○ wake
- ○ sleeping

For questions 2 to 6, which word completes the sentence correctly?

2 **Penny is the _____ runner in her class.**

- ○ fast
- ○ faster
- ○ fastest

3 **It is nearly the last day of _____ week.**

- ○ a
- ○ an
- ○ the

4 **It is bad luck to walk _____ a ladder.**

- ○ on
- ○ under
- ○ through
- ○ between

5 **Dana got good marks _____ she studied.**

- ○ if
- ○ unless
- ○ until
- ○ because

6 **Leanne likes swimming _____ not diving.**

- ○ and
- ○ but
- ○ if
- ○ once

7 **Which sentence is a command?**

- ○ Summer is my favourite season.
- ○ Do you like sushi?
- ○ I can't believe you won!
- ○ Pick up this mess!

8 **Which sentence is a question?**

- ○ What time is it?
- ○ Tell me the time!
- ○ It is five o'clock.
- ○ I'm so excited!

BOB time!

CAPITAL LETTERS and FULL STOPS

PUNCTUATION

Capital letter ABC

When starting a sentence.

When using proper nouns.

Full stop .

When ending most sentences.

Capital letters and full stops show where sentences start and finish.

Proper nouns are words that name **specific** people and places.

Ian, Sydney, Nielsen Street

The names of days and months are also proper nouns, and should start with a capital letter. The names of holidays also start with a capital letter.

Sunday, March, Easter

The personal pronoun "I", is always a capital, even if it has been contracted.

I've, I'll, I'm

Capital letters and full stops are highlighted in this text.

My family and **I** are going overseas for **C**hristmas this year**. W**e are going to **S**cotland to see **M**um's parents**. T**hey live in **I**nverness, which is near the **L**och **N**ess **M**onster!
Mum thinks it will snow and we will have a white **C**hristmas**. M**y brother **W**illiam and **I** will have snowball fights and we will make snowmen**. W**e will also try to see the monster, but **D**ad thinks it will be too cold**. H**e says the monster goes south for winter**.**

Which two words should begin with a capital letter? Shade TWO bubbles.

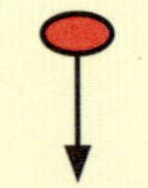
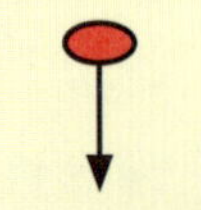
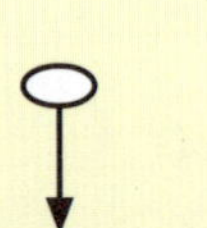
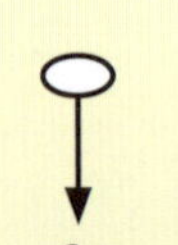

we are going to india to visit my family.

We practise

You practise

Which two words should begin with a capital letter? Shade TWO bubbles in each question.

1 "my teacher's name is mr Davison," Joanne said.

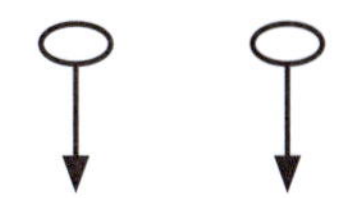

2 Fiona is moving into a new house on baker street.

3 My cousin john is coming to my place on sunday.

4 I'm going to england for christmas next year.

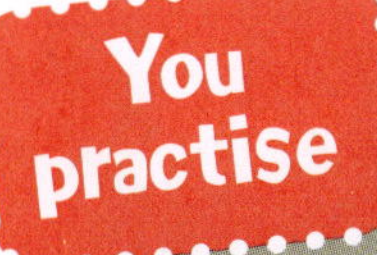

You practise

Which sentence has the correct punctuation? Shade ONE bubble in each question.

5
- ○ My favourite country is Australia it is a good place to live.
- ○ My favourite Country is australia it is a good place. To live.
- ○ My favourite country is australia. It is a good place to live.
- ○ My favourite country is Australia. It is a good place to live.

6
- ○ I went to greece last year. The scenery was beautiful.
- ○ I went to Greece last year. The scenery was beautiful.
- ○ I went to Greece. Last year the scenery was beautiful.
- ○ I went to greece. last year the scenery was beautiful.

7
- ○ I went to the supermarket with Mum. She bought me a chocolate.
- ○ I went to the Supermarket with Mum she bought me a chocolate.
- ○ I went to the Supermarket with mum. she bought me a chocolate.
- ○ I went to the supermarket with mum. She bought me a chocolate.

8
- ○ Little Jim dropped his Ice Cream. He cried a lot.
- ○ Little Jim dropped his ice cream. He cried a lot.
- ○ Little jim dropped his ice cream he cried a lot.
- ○ Little Jim dropped his ice cream He cried a lot.

UNIT 18

QUESTION MARKS and EXCLAMATION MARKS

Question mark ?

At the end of a direct question
e.g. *What did you have for lunch?*

Not used for indirect questions
e.g. *I asked you what you had for lunch.*

Exclamation mark !

Used for commands or orders that need something to be done, e.g. *Tie your shoelaces!*
Used for **exclamations**—sentences that show strong feelings, e.g. *My dog is missing!*

Exclamation marks sound like someone is shouting!

Question marks and exclamation marks are highlighted in this text.

Do you believe in ghosts? I didn't … until last week.

I went on holiday with my family to a small seaside town. We stayed in a big, old hotel, far away from the centre of town. We were the only guests, which I thought was strange. It didn't take long to find out why!

"Did you say something?" Mum asked, while we were unpacking.

"No. Why?"

"Oh, nothing," Mum said. "I thought I heard someone groaning."

"Bags, this is my bed!" my sister Sue shouted, and leapt on the bed by the window.

I was just about to argue when she shrieked and fell off the bed.

"Hah! Serves you right," I said.

"Did you see that?" Sue asked, her whole body shaking. "There was someone sitting on that bed!"

I looked, but there was no one there. At first I thought Sue had gone crazy, but that night I found out she was telling the truth!

Shade ONE bubble to show where the missing question mark (?) should go.

"Who likes watching scary movies " Carl asked

Shade ONE bubble to show where the missing question mark (?) should go.

1 "Is that your sandwich ○ ○ " ○ Connie ○ asked ○

2 The teacher asked ○ "Does anyone have a note ○ to hand in today ○ ○ "

Shade ONE bubble to show where the missing exclamation mark (!) should go.

3 "Call the police ○ quickly ○ ○ " Dylan ordered ○

4 Marion shouted ○ "I'm so happy I won ○ first prize ○ ○ "

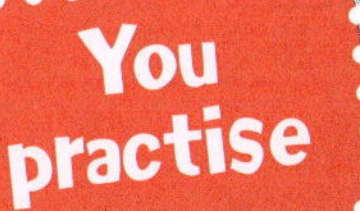

Which sentence has the correct punctuation? Shade ONE bubble in each question.

5
- ○ "I want to go home" Francis cried!
- ○ "I want to go home!" Francis cried.
- ○ "I want to go home"! Francis cried.
- ○ "I want to go home?" Francis cried.

6
- ○ "Do you want a glass of milk?" Mum asked.
- ○ "Do you want a glass of milk" Mum asked?
- ○ "Do you want a glass of milk!" Mum asked.
- ○ "Do you want a glass of milk"? Mum asked.

7
- ○ "Catch the ball" the coach shouted!
- ○ "Catch the ball" the coach shouted?
- ○ "Catch the ball?" the coach shouted.
- ○ "Catch the ball!" the coach shouted.

BOB time!

COMMAS

Comma ,

When pausing in a sentence.

To separate items in a list.

To separate lists of adjectives.

To separate clauses in a sentence.

Place a comma between items in a list. Make sure you use the word 'and' before the last item in the list. You do not need to place a comma before the 'and'.

I went to the store and bought flour, sugar, eggs and butter.

Place a comma between two or more adjectives that describe a noun. The comma is used instead of the word 'and'. If there are three or more adjectives, use the word 'and' before the last item.

We live in a blue and white house.

We live in a big, blue and white house.

Clauses are groups of words that contain a subject (a person or thing that does something) and a verb (an action). **Commas can be used to separate clauses** where there is a pause between them.

Unless Julie hurries up, she will be late for the show.

Read the sentence out loud and consider inserting a comma where you need to take a breath.

We practise

Where does the missing comma (,) go? Shade ONE bubble in each question.

My favourite lunch is a peanut ○ butter ● banana ○ and ○ honey sandwich.

The plump ● happy ○ baby ○ pulled my ○ nose.

Because ○ it was raining ● we ○ did not go ○ to the park.

You practise

Where does the missing comma (,) go?
Shade ONE bubble in each question.

I want to eat ○ some cake ○ but ○ it is ○ all gone.

Unless you tie ○ your shoelaces ○ you ○ will ○ trip over.

The Australian ○ flag is ○ red ○ white ○ and blue.

The long ○ windy ○ and steep road ○ came to ○ an abrupt end.

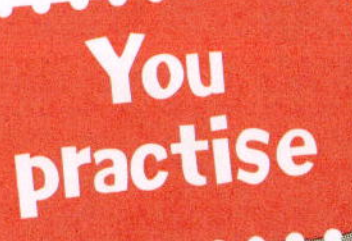

Which sentence has the correct punctuation?
Shade ONE bubble in each question.

- ○ I am going shopping with Mum Dad, and Ben.
- ○ I am going shopping with Mum, Dad and Ben.
- ○ I am going shopping, with Mum Dad and Ben.
- ○ I am going shopping with, Mum Dad and Ben.

- ○ The deep, dark cave was very damp.
- ○ The deep dark, cave was very damp.
- ○ The deep dark cave, was very damp.
- ○ The deep dark cave was, very damp.

- ○ The sky was cloudy but, it was still very hot.
- ○ The sky was cloudy but it was still, very hot.
- ○ The sky, was cloudy but it was still very hot.
- ○ The sky was cloudy, but it was still very hot.

BOB time!

UNIT 20

MORE COMMAS

Comma ,

When pausing in a sentence.

To separate words, phrases and clauses that interrupt the flow of a sentence.

To separate direct speech from the rest of the text.

Commas make complicated sentences easier to understand.

When a group of words—**phrase** or **clause**—is inserted into a sentence, commas are used like brackets to separate those words from the rest of the sentence. One comma is placed **before**, and one is placed **after** the group of words.

My brother, **who is five years old**, *is starting school next year.*

comma clause comma

Direct speech refers to words spoken out loud. It is placed in quotation marks, and is separated from other parts of the text by using commas.

"It's not as hard as it sounds," *she said.*

speech comma

He replied, **"Oh yes it is!"**

comma speech

The same rule applies to longer sentences.

"Just stand still," he said, "while I take your photograph."

We practise

Where does the missing comma (,) go? Shade ONE bubble.

"I'm learning to knit " Shane said.

Where do the missing commas (,) go? Shade TWO bubbles.

"I'm learning to knit " Shane said "so I can make myself a scarf."

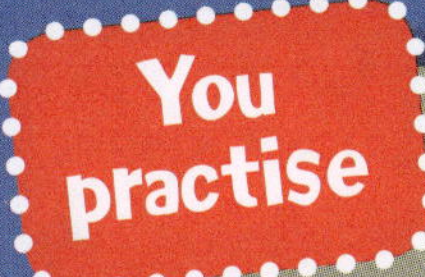

Where does the missing comma (,) go? Shade ONE bubble in each question.

1 "What a lovely ◯ painting ◯ ◯ " Grandpa ◯ said.

2 Gianni shouted ◯ "Don't go ◯ without me ◯ ◯ "

Where do the missing commas (,) go? Shade TWO bubbles in each question.

3 "I'd like to tell you ◯ ◯ " Brian said ◯ "but I don't know the answer ◯ "

4 My brother ◯ who is allergic to peanuts ◯ has to be ◯ careful ◯ with what he eats.

You practise

Which sentence has the correct punctuation? Shade ONE bubble in each question.

5
- ◯ "Come and get it" he said.
- ◯ "Come and get it," he said.
- ◯ "Come and get it", he said.
- ◯ "Come and, get it" he said.

6
- ◯ Sharon said, "I like your haircut."
- ◯ Sharon, said "I like your haircut."
- ◯ Sharon said "I like your haircut."
- ◯ Sharon said "I like your haircut,"

7
- ◯ "This time" Kyle said "it's for real."
- ◯ "This time," Kyle said "it's for real."
- ◯ "This time" Kyle said, "it's for real."
- ◯ "This time," Kyle said, "it's for real."

8
- ◯ I am as you can see tall for my age.
- ◯ I am, as you can see, tall for my age.
- ◯ I am as, you can see, tall for my age.
- ◯ I am as you can see, tall for my age.

Now try the punctuation test on page 60!

BOB time!

SPEECH MARKS

Speech marks are used to show that a person or character is speaking.

Speech marks always come in pairs and they look like this:

“ when someone starts talking, and ” after they finish.

Speech marks are only used for direct speech, that is, for actual words spoken.

“It’s nice to meet you,” Stanley said.

They are **not** used when someone is thinking.

Stanley thought it was nice to meet Zoe.

They are also **not** used where a character is not actually talking.

Stanley told Zoe that it was nice to meet her.

Direct speech starts with a capital letter, even if the speech begins part way through a sentence.

Stanley said to Zoe, “It’s nice to meet you.”

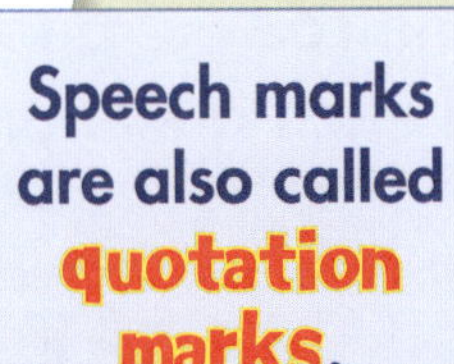

Which sentence needs speech marks?
Shade ONE bubble in each question.

We practise

- ● Would you like an apple? Greg asked.
- ○ Greg asked Cheryl if she wanted an apple.

- ○ Cheryl wanted to know whether he meant a red or green apple.
- ● Red or green? Cheryl replied.

- ○ Greg didn’t see how it mattered. He rolled his eyes.
- ● Greg rolled his eyes. Does it matter? he muttered.

Which sentence needs speech marks? Shade ONE bubble in each question.

1
- ⬭ What time is it? Marina asked.
- ⬭ Marina wondered what the time was.
- ⬭ Marina asked Kelly if she knew the time.

2
- ⬭ It is half past two, Kelly said.
- ⬭ Kelly looked at her watch and saw it was half past two.
- ⬭ Kelly told Marina that it was half past two.

3
- ⬭ Mum called out that dinner was ready.
- ⬭ Mum shouted, Dinner's ready!
- ⬭ Mum thought that dinner was ready.

4
- ⬭ I asked Mum what we were having for dinner.
- ⬭ I wonder what we are having for dinner.
- ⬭ What's for dinner? I asked.

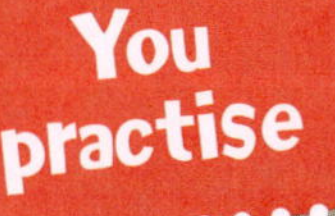

Which sentence has the correct punctuation? Shade ONE bubble in each question.

5
- ⬭ "It's time for bed," Dad said.
- ⬭ "It's time for bed, Dad said."
- ⬭ Dad told us that it was "time for bed".

6
- ⬭ "Please shut the door, Carly said."
- ⬭ "Please shut the door," Carly said.
- ⬭ Carly asked me to "shut the door".

7
- ⬭ The teacher "asked did you bring your note?"
- ⬭ The teacher asked, "Did you bring your note?"
- ⬭ The teacher asked me "whether I brought my note."

8
- ⬭ Ben wants to play "Simon Says."
- ⬭ Ben said, "Let's play," Simon Says!
- ⬭ Ben said, "Let's play Simon Says!"

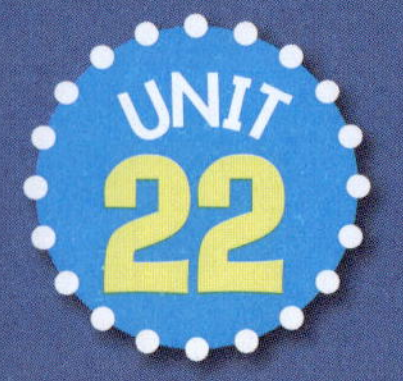

MORE SPEECH MARKS

Speech marks " " are used to show that a person or character is speaking.

They are placed at the start and end of the **direct speech** – that is, the actual words spoken.

Punctuation for the speaker's words, such as commas, full stops and question marks, goes **inside** the speech marks.

The speaker's name goes **outside** the quotation marks, either before or after the spoken words.

"Like this," Mei said.

Mei added, "And like this."

Did you notice the comma before the spoken words in the second example?
Commas are used to introduce direct speech where the spoken words are not at the start of the sentence.

If the spoken sentence ends with an exclamation mark or a question mark, don't add a comma as well.

"There's no need for a comma here!" Mei shouted.

Don't add extra punctuation directly after the quotation marks.

We practise

Shade TWO bubbles to show where the missing speech marks (" ") should go.

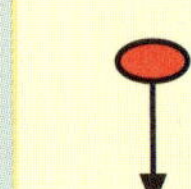

I had a very strange dream last night , Safa said.

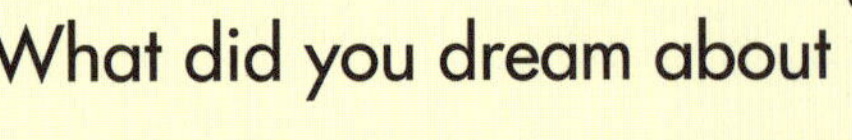

What did you dream about ? Mum asked .

"I can't remember all of it , Safa said , but in one part, I was flying."

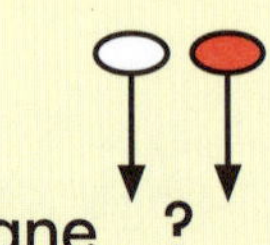

Mum asked, Do you mean in an aeroplane ?

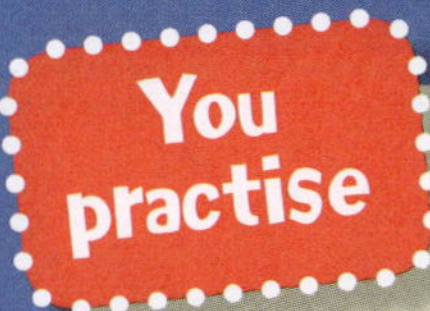

Shade TWO bubbles in each question to show where the missing speech marks (" ") should go.

It's my birthday next week , Hannah said .

Sam asked, How was your weekend ?

Ring for an ambulance ! Jim shouted.

Maureen said, I think it's going to rain .

Which sentence has the correct punctuation?
Shade ONE bubble in each question.

- ○ "This is my favourite book" Mustafa said.
- ○ "This is my favourite book," Mustafa said.
- ○ "This is my favourite book, Mustafa said."
- ○ "This is my favourite book, Mustafa said".

- ○ "What time are you coming back? Freda asked."
- ○ "What time are you coming back Freda asked?"
- ○ "What time are you coming back?" Freda asked.
- ○ "What time are you coming back"? Freda asked.

- ○ Tara said "I took my dog for a walk today."
- ○ "Tara said I took my dog for a walk today."
- ○ Tara said "I took my dog for a walk today".
- ○ Tara said, "I took my dog for a walk today."

- ○ Li asked? "Have you seen my bag."
- ○ Li asked, "Have you seen my bag."?
- ○ Li asked, "Have you seen my bag?"
- ○ "Li asked Have you seen my bag?"

BOB time!

APOSTROPHES for CONTRACTIONS

Contractions are words that have been shortened. They are usually two words combined into one word. The new word is quicker and easier to say and write, but its meaning does not change.

do + not = *don't*

we + will = *we'll*

I + have = *I've*

Say the contraction out loud to hear which letters have been removed.

Avoid this common trap: **It's** is a contraction of **it + is**. It is **not** used to show ownership.

An apostrophe ' is used to show that the word is a contraction. It is put in the exact place where the letters have been left out.

I + will the *'wi'* is removed and replaced with an apostrophe

I'll

Contractions are used in informal language, for example, when friends or relatives talk to each other. They are also used when people write letters and emails to friends and family.

Shade ONE bubble to show where the missing apostrophe (') should go.

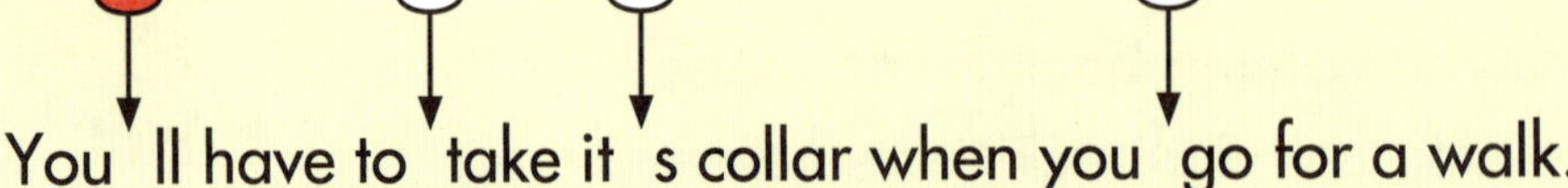

You ll have to take it s collar when you go for a walk.

Shade ONE bubble to show your answer.
Which word or words could be repaced with you're?

- ○ your are
- ● you are
- ○ you were

Which sentence uses the apostrophe (') correctly? Shade ONE bubble.

- ○ I'd better help you bath the big dog because its fur is' so thick.
- ○ I'd better help you bath the big dog because it's fur is so thick.
- ● I'd better help you bath the big dog because its fur is so thick.

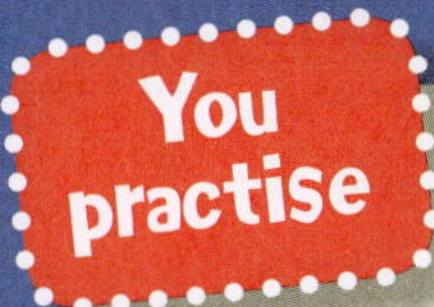

Shade ONE bubble in each question to show where the missing apostrophe (') should go.

Chris ○ says ○ he ○ ll start so ○ on.

This ○ is ○ n ○ t very fun ○ ny.

You ○ re going to do well at the sport ○ s ○ carnival this ○ year.

I wouldn ○ t take it ○ s ○ bone if I ○ were you!

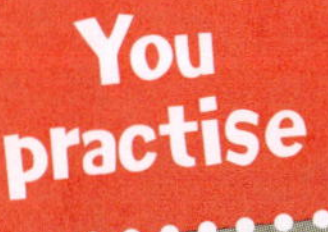

Shade ONE bubble in each question to show your answer.

Which word or words could be replaced with we'll?

- ○ wheel
- ○ we have
- ○ we are well
- ○ we will

Which word or words could be replaced with I've?

- ○ hive
- ○ I have
- ○ I will
- ○ I would have

Which sentence uses the apostrophe (') correctly? Shade ONE bubble in each question.

- ○ You're invited to my birthday party.
- ○ Your'e invited to my birthday party.
- ○ Youre invited to my b'thday party.
- ○ Your invited to my birthday party.

- ○ Shes' welcome to stay with us.
- ○ She's welcome to stay with us.
- ○ She's welcome to stay with us'.
- ○ Shes welcome to stay with us'.

BOB time!

APOSTROPHES for POSSESSION

Possession, or ownership, means something belongs to a person or thing. In sentences, the person or thing is a noun (e.g. *boy*), proper noun (e.g. *Jack*) or pronoun (e.g. *you*).

Jack's book The book belongs to Jack.

Possession is shown by using an apostrophe ' and adding the letter 's' at the end of the noun. The apostrophe comes **between** the noun and the 's'.

Jane's cat The cat belongs to Jane.

The cat's toys The toys belong to the cat.

If there is more than one owner and the plural noun ends with 's', the apostrophe is placed **after** the 's'.

The cats' toys The toys belong to the cats (plural cats).

If the noun is singular, but ends with 's', the apostrophe is placed **after** the 's'.

James' cat The cat belongs to James.

Avoid this common trap: Don't confuse plurals with possession.

Look at the cute babies.
"Babies" is plural.

Look at the baby's cot.
"Baby's" shows possession.

Where does the missing apostrophe (') go? Shade ONE bubble in each question.

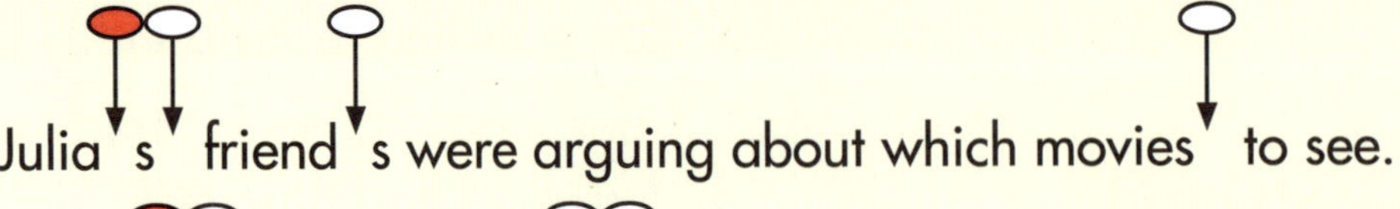

Julia s friend s were arguing about which movies to see.

Stavro s cat had kitten s .

Chri s dog had puppie s .

The boy s bedroom s were very messy.

We practise

Don't use an apostrophe just because a word ends in 's'.

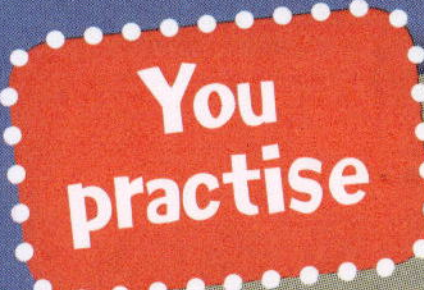

Where does the missing apostrophe (') go?
Shade ONE bubble in each question.

1 Where is Greg s school bag?

2 The dog s played in Sam s garden.

3 I took the toy s back to Kim s house.

4 The girl s toilets were closed during the holiday s .

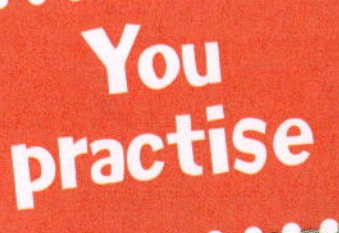

Which sentence uses the apostrophe (') correctly?
Shade ONE bubble in each question.

5
- ○ The boys shirt was too big.
- ○ The boy's shirt was too big.
- ○ The boys' shirt was too big.
- ○ The boys shirt was' too big.

6
- ○ The boys shirts were too big.
- ○ The boys shirt's were too big.
- ○ The boys' shirts were too big.
- ○ The boys shirts' were too big.

7
- ○ Fresh juicy apple's for sale.
- ○ Fresh juicy apples' for sale.
- ○ Fresh juicy apples for sale.
- ○ Fresh juicy' apples for sale.

8
- ○ It's guarding its kennel.
- ○ Its guarding its kennel.
- ○ It's guarding it's kennel.
- ○ Its guarding it's kennel.

Now try the punctuation test on page 61 !

BOB time!

You practise

PUNCTUATION TEST 1

Do this test after completing Unit 20. Spend no more than 6 minutes on this test.

1 **Which two words should begin with a capital letter? Shade TWO bubbles.**

our new teacher's name is mr Johnson.

2 **Where does the missing comma (,) go? Shade ONE bubble.**

We put ham cheese and tomatoes on the pizza.

3 **Where does the missing comma (,) go? Shade ONE bubble.**

"I'm going for a swim today " Sasha said.

4 **Where do the missing commas (,) go? Shade TWO bubbles.**

My sister who is twelve is going to high school.

Which sentence has the correct punctuation?
Shade ONE bubble in each question.

5
- ○ The sun is coming up. It is Wednesday morning.
- ○ The sun is coming up. It is wednesday morning.
- ○ The sun is coming up It is wednesday morning.
- ○ The sun is coming up it is. Wednesday morning.

6
- ○ We had eggs, bacon and sausages for breakfast.
- ○ We had eggs bacon, and sausages for breakfast.
- ○ We had eggs bacon and sausages, for breakfast.
- ○ We had, eggs bacon and sausages for breakfast.

7
- ○ My cousin who lives, in New Zealand, is coming to visit.
- ○ My cousin, who lives in New Zealand is coming, to visit.
- ○ My cousin, who lives in New Zealand, is coming to visit.
- ○ My cousin who lives, in New Zealand is coming, to visit.

8 **Which sentence requires speech marks? Shade ONE bubble.**
- ○ Are you ready yet? Dad asked.
- ○ Dad wanted to know if we were ready.
- ○ Dad asked us if we were ready.

BOB time!

PUNCTUATION TEST 2

Do this test after completing Unit 24. Spend no more than 6 minutes on this test.

1 **Where do the missing speech marks (" ") go? Shade TWO bubbles.**

What's your name ? Nicholas asked

2 **Shade ONE bubble to show where the missing question mark (?) should go.**

"Have you seen my new little kitten " Alexi asked

3 **Shade ONE bubble to show where the missing apostrophe (') should go.**

I can t believe you do not like egg s .

4 **Shade ONE bubble to show where the missing apostrophe (') should go.**

We are going to Chris house to meet his cousin s .

Which sentence has the correct punctuation?

Shade ONE bubble in each question.

5
- ○ "Turn the music down, Mum said".
- ○ "Turn the music down," Mum said.
- ○ "Turn the music down", Mum said.
- ○ "Turn the music down Mum", said.

6
- ○ "Careful you don't fall down that hole!" Rebecca shouted.
- ○ "Careful you don't fall down that hole"! Rebecca shouted.
- ○ "Careful you don't fall down that hole," Rebecca shouted!
- ○ "Careful you don't fall down that hole,"! Rebecca shouted.

7
- ○ Its not my fault you fell down the stair's.
- ○ Its not my fault you fell down the stairs'.
- ○ It's not my fault you fell down the stairs'.
- ○ It's not my fault you fell down the stairs.

8
- ○ Thoma's sisters are going to a birthday party.
- ○ Thomas' sisters are going to a birthday party.
- ○ Thomas sister's are going to a birthday party.
- ○ Thomas sisters' are going to a birthday party.

BOB time!

ANSWERS

Pre-test

1 thief
2 bridge
3 thoughtless
4 mistakes
5 haircut
6 he
7 catch
8 fly
9 strongest
10 under
11 but
12 It is Sharon's birthday tomorrow. Are you going to the party?
13 My best friends are Vicky, Jia and Susan.
14 "It's too hot in here," Dean said.
15 Michelle's

Unit 1

1 around
2 thief
3 queen
4 float
5 deceived
6 house
7 stove
8 here
9 relief
10 quiet

Unit 2

1 witch
2 baby
3 cage
4 sticks
5 cry
6 truck
7 itch
8 judge
9 sky
10 happy

Unit 3

1 should
2 wrapper
3 electrician
4 motion
5 tough
6 caution
7 trough
8 knight
9 addition
10 wrist

Unit 4

1 unseen
2 disagree
3 dislikes
4 unzipped
5 replay
6 rewrite
7 mistake
8 deflate
9 unlocked
10 untidy

Unit 5

1 cleaning
2 hopeless
3 cheerful
4 ugliest
5 hopeful
6 sadly
7 funniest
8 dresses
9 turning
10 brightly

Unit 6

1 teeth
2 babies
3 geese
4 toys
5 beaches
6 coaches
7 flies
8 quizzes
9 toothbrushes
10 keys

Unit 7

1 meat
2 knew
3 blew
4 break
5 by
6 ate
7 stare
8 pear
9 flu
10 heard

Unit 8

1 rattlesnake
2 watermelon
3 skateboard
4 sandpaper
5 daylight
6 something
7 bedroom
8 raincoat
9 homesick
10 nightlight

Spelling test 1

1 ceiling
2 boat
3 sandwich
4 station
5 enough
6 believe
7 make
8 monkey
9 through
10 knee

Spelling test 2

1 weekly
2 speechless
3 bushes
4 band
5 milkshake
6 painful
7 enjoyable
8 won
9 witches
10 sunflowers

Unit 9

1 Pavlo
2 leopard
3 worry
4 Japan
5 he
6 Canberra
7 they

ANSWERS

Unit 10

1 whistling
2 was
3 heard
4 have
5 walked
6 rolled
7 shouted

Unit 11

1 fell
2 is coming
3 ride
4 swam
5 is doing
6 caught
7 broke
8 will be
9 is playing
10 flew

Unit 12

1 run
2 is
3 was
4 drink
5 tastes
6 am
7 is
8 are
9 were
10 hop

Unit 13

1 smaller
2 smallest
3 short
4 shorter
5 shortest
6 gently
7 carefully
8 hard
9 harder
10 hardest

Unit 14

1 over
2 into
3 between
4 under
5 on
6 the
7 a
8 by
9 on
10 under

Unit 15

1 and
2 unless
3 or
4 because
5 or
6 so
7 but
8 if

Unit 16

1 Wash your hands!
2 Do it now!
3 I won first prize!
4 I saw a ghost!
5 Where does Jim live?
6 What is your favourite colour?
7 My dog's name is Sam.
8 Mum is baking bread.

Grammar test 1

1 Street
2 sang
3 I should have listened to you.
4 its
5 helped
6 write
7 eats
8 was

Grammar test 2

1 carefully
2 fastest
3 the
4 under
5 because
6 but
7 Pick up this mess!
8 What time is it?

Unit 17

1 My Mr
2 Baker Street
3 John Sunday
4 England Christmas
5 My favourite country is Australia. It is a good place to live.
6 I went to Greece last year. The scenery was beautiful.
7 I went to the supermarket with Mum. She bought me a chocolate.
8 Little Jim dropped his ice cream. He cried a lot.

Unit 18

1 sandwich?"
2 today?"
3 quickly!"
4 prize!"
5 "I want to go home!" Francis cried.
6 "Do you want a glass of milk?" Mum asked.
7 "Catch the ball!" the coach shouted.

Unit 19

1 cake,
2 shoelaces,
3 red,
4 long,
5 I am going shopping with Mum, Dad and Ben.
6 The deep, dark cave was very damp.
7 The sky was cloudy, but it was still very hot.

Unit 20

1 painting,"
2 shouted,
3 you," said,
4 brother, peanuts,
5 "Come and get it," he said.
6 Sharon said, "I like your haircut."
7 "This time," Kyle said, "it's for real."
8 I am, as you can see, tall for my age.

ANSWERS

Unit 21

1 What time is it? Marina asked.
2 It is half past two, Kelly said.
3 Mum shouted, Dinner's ready!
4 What's for dinner? I asked.
5 "It's time for bed," Dad said.
6 "Please shut the door," Carly said.
7 The teacher asked, "Did you bring your note?"
8 Ben said, "Let's play Simon Says!"

Unit 22

1 "It's ... week,"
2 "How ... weekend?"
3 "Ring ... ambulance!"
4 "I ... rain."
5 "This is my favourite book," Mustafa said.
6 "What time are you coming back?" Freda asked.
7 Tara said, "I took my dog for a walk today."
8 Li asked, "Have you seen my bag?"

Unit 23

1 he'll
2 isn't
3 you're
4 wouldn't
5 we will
6 I have
7 You're invited to my birthday party.
8 She's welcome to stay with us.

Unit 24

1 Greg's
2 Sam's
3 Kim's
4 girls'
5 The boy's shirt was too big.
6 The boys' shirts were too big.
7 Fresh juicy apples for sale.
8 It's guarding its kennel.

Punctuation test 1

1 Our Mr
2 ham,
3 today,"
4 sister, twelve,
5 The sun is coming up. It is Wednesday morning.
6 We had eggs, bacon and sausages for breakfast.
7 My cousin, who lives in New Zealand, is coming to visit.
8 Are you ready yet? Dad asked.

Punctuation test 2

1 "What's ... name?"
2 kitten?"
3 can't
4 Chris'
5 "Turn the music down," Mum said.
6 "Careful you don't fall down that hole!" Rebecca shouted.
7 It's not my fault you fell down the stairs.
8 Thomas' sisters are going to a birthday party.

Sample NAPLAN test

1 house
2 sick
3 rough
4 lamb
5 distaste
6 helpful
7 torches
8 ate
9 stopwatch
10 receive
11 edge
12 station
13 wrote
14 unplug
15 brightly
16 bushes
17 break
18 sunset
19 hopped
20 quickly
21 your
22 write
23 laugh
24 the
25 in
26 because
27 Did you say thank you?
28 Rachel has a new pet dog. She will call him Sandy.
29 over,
30 chocolate,
31 "The dog ate my cheeseburger," Jamie said.
32 Leo asked, "Are you going to finish that?"
33 presents!
34 Christmas?"
35 Pam wouldn't like to lose her pencils.
36 Are those Pam's pencils?